F

C000132987

"Paintner takes us on a pilgrimage to discover the holiness of the natural world. One long section features stories of Christian saints who had a kinship with animals—herons, ravens, hares, cats, otters. These poems are both charming and whimsical, filled with a sense of divine presence that we have lost in the modern electronic world. In another section, she weaves Irish myths and legends and traditional fairy tales like an intricately laced Celtic knot. Anyone interested in the intersection of poetry, Celtic mythology, and spirituality will surely love this beautiful book as much as I did."
—**Barbara Crooker**, poet, author of *The Book of Kells* and *Some Glad Morning*

"An inspiring, luscious, deep delve into Earth Wisdom and lively tales of Christian saints; a spirited and intimate re-seeing of the desert mystics and beloved St. Francis and Julian of Norwich, offering their transcendent wisdom. Lyrical poems of praise and jubilation, of kinship with animals and our inner wild, surprising poems of the ecstatic ordinary—poems to gladden the heart, make spirits soar, and invite the soul to linger long in gentle quiet."
—**Judyth Hill**, poet, author of *Dazzling Wobble* and *A Presence of Angels*

"Poems come in two types: those that reflect the poet, and poems that transcend the poet. Both can touch you; only the second can transform you. Christine Valters Paintner's *The Wisdom of Wild Grace* is the latter. Don't simply read the words, listen to the message. And dare to be transformed."
—**Rabbi Rami Shapiro**, poet, author of *Accidental Grace: Poems*

"The poet intends these poems to be invitations, and they are: invitations to know ourselves better by seeing the world more clearly through the eyes of one who loves it fiercely. It is a wonderful, wonder full collection."
—**Bonnie Thurston**, poet, author of *O Taste and See* and *Practicing Silence*

St. Gall and the Bear

The Wisdom of Wild Grace

poems

Christine Valters Paintner

PARACLETE PRESS
BREWSTER, MASSACHUSETTS

2020 First Printing

The Wisdom of Wild Grace: Poems

Text copyright © 2020 by Christine Valters Paintner
Illustrations copyright © 2020 by David Hollington, http://davidhollington.co.uk

ISBN 978-1-64060-558-9

The Paraclete Press name and logo (dove on cross) are trademarks of Paraclete Press, Inc.

Library of Congress Cataloging-in-Publication Data

Names: Paintner, Christine Valters, author.
Title: The wisdom of wild grace : poems / Christine Valters Paintner ;
   illustrations by David Hollington.
Description: Brewster, Massachusetts : Paraclete Press, [2020] | Summary:
   "These illustrated poems are a doorway to our inner wilderness, to be
   present to what we discover beyond our neatly controlled worlds"—
   Provided by publisher.
Identifiers: LCCN 2020015881 (print) | LCCN 2020015882 (ebook) | ISBN
   9781640605589 (trade paperback) | ISBN 9781640605596 (epub) | ISBN
   9781640605633 (pdf)
Subjects: LCGFT: Poetry.
Classification: LCC PS3616.A337848 W57 2020 (print) | LCC PS3616.A337848
   (ebook) | DDC 811/.6—dc23
LC record available at https://lccn.loc.gov/2020015881
LC ebook record available at https://lccn.loc.gov/2020015882

10 9 8 7 6 5 4 3 2 1

All rights reserved. No portion of this book may be reproduced, stored in an electronic
retrieval system, or transmitted in any form or by any means—electronic, mechanical,
photocopy, recording, or any other—except for brief quotations in printed reviews, without
the prior permission of the publisher.

Published by Paraclete Press
Brewster, Massachusetts
www.paracletepress.com

Printed in China

Contents •

Writing Wild

Myths and Fairy Tales

The Wild Self

Closing

Introduction •

These poems are invitations.

When I long for expansiveness and connection to something far greater than my own daily concerns and struggles, a walk by the sea or in the forest expands me.

We live in a time when Earth is threatened on so many fronts by human development. Slowly we seem to be awakening to the truth that our personal well-being is intimately woven together with the well-being of all creatures and plants. Many of us might have been taught by our religious traditions that humans have dominion over nature or that animals don't feel pain or have souls.

The more we cultivate our own intimacy with the wild, the more we open to different truth. Wildness doesn't mean we have to go out into the forest or travel long ways; the wild is a place within us.

Each poem here is a doorway into this inner wilderness, a call to sit and be present to what we discover beyond the borders of our neatly controlled worlds. Wildness is vulnerable, risky, spacious, and full of possibility. And this is where I invite you to sit and rest awhile and dwell with me. . . .

I have long loved the stories of Christian saints who had a kinship with animals. They come mostly from the early Christian desert and Celtic traditions, but also feature later medieval saints such as St. Francis of Assisi and St. Julian of Norwich.

Ever since I was a child, animals have offered me a window into an aspect of the divine presence that is more intuitive, more instinctual, wilder. The monastic tradition held the conviction that this kind of connection and friendship with the animal world was a sign of holiness at work.

The heart of this collection is a series of poems inspired by the stories of animal and saint connections. I meditated with each story to listen to what it might reveal. Each story felt like a way into a new or renewed way of being in the world where nature is an intimate guide and companion. These stories remind me of some of the old fairy tales that hold wisdom for how to live well if we pay close enough attention.

Many of the other poems in this collection are inspired by the tradition of the psalms of creation, those prayers of praise that celebrate how everything conspires to share joy and gratitude for this beautiful world.

What we need most right now is a revolution of love. We desperately need to fall in love with creation so that everything we do reflects this love. If reading these poems supports you to see the world in a new way, to make time to sit outside and cherish the breezes, or to fall more in love, then my heart is full of gratitude and gladness.

The Wisdom of Wild Grace

You Are Here
(after Rainer Maria Rilke's Book of Hours*)*

You are the now and not-yet, the darkened dawn just before
the first rays rise and you are the rays that pierce and prod.

You are the siren screeching through city streets
dropping me to my knees in prayer.

You are the lilac and the dust,
the refugee's body found on shore with empty pockets.

You are the wound that does not heal, the salve,
the bandage, and the raised scar that remains.

You are the dandelion growing through concrete cracks,
the mirror smashed into pieces, the mosaic created.

You are the vigil for my mother dying, you are the steady beep
of the heartrate monitor and the long tone that makes me wail.

You are ash from the burning towers
the great gashed tree felled by storm, now moss-coated, silent.

You are the gray headstone and the red bird that lands and
       sings,
the gaunt face I ignore while rushing down the street.

You are the old man's spectacles
and the love letters from his wife now gone.

You are thick grime, a sob stuck in the throat,
the voice long silent speaking once again.

Original Poetry
(after Moya Cannon)

The mountains stand
as guardians of eternity
against a mottled sky,
the tide withdraws,
then turns, approaches me
like a shy lover,
each morning the sun
appears once again
and buttercups open
their lemon mouths to sing
of light and I can almost believe
resurrection is possible,
can almost see the world is a poem
hiding under the fragile stem
of flower that bows at the force
of the coming storm.

St. Hildegard Gives Her Writing Advice

Cry out and write,
were the words you heard
tumble toward you from
the blue-spattered sky
midway through your life,

Follow the greening,
you tell me in dreams
and I reach for the thread
which slips from my
close-clutched hand
on fine days.

How? I plead,
you show me my dog
playing in the sunlight,
the way shadows sashay
across my desk, and the orchid
holds out her purple tongue.

Always make time for tea,
you utter as you take me
by the hand through the garden,
show me dandelion and thistle,
yarrow and sage, *sipping*
slows you down so you can see.

Listen to the flowers teach,
you whisper,
find a meadow, lie down,
and wait for the poem to arrive,
I scoff and sigh
then find myself

among marigold, long
grasses, and loosestrife
all singing their glee
and my page is full
before I remember how
I resisted coming here at all.

Aubade

The day opens its white page,
spreading herself like so much possibility,
you take your pen, pausing
before you begin so you can hear
the jackdaw caw high above
your tiny shadow and the snowdrop's
insistent blooming, somewhere
is the knowing glance of badger,
each unafraid to write their stories
on wind and soil and you see they
offer ink for your pen in
a hundred different colors.

Praise Be

"O tell us poet, what is it you do?—I praise."
—Rainer Maria Rilke

Praise be the words that spill and splash like a river
across granite, smoothing rough edges and singing of time
always moving, offering the thirsty world a drink.

Praise be the nouns that root us here on earth:
lemon and lilac, worm and wolf, your lips
and your hands, a paw print in the sand.

Praise be the places where poems hide:
the drawer of old socks, the kitchen window,
the dusty picture frame, and the keychain.

Praise be the verbs that invite us to new places
as we wiggle, wonder, wander, and wish,
flail, flagellate, flower, and fish.

Praise be the spaces between words that pause us
interrupt our headlong quest to arrive at some imagined future,
ask us to be a guest of this moment now.

Praise be the lines from poems that rise up
in the dark, meet me in my sorrow and shame
to bring a lantern, a working latch in the rusty gate.

I Greet the Muse

I met my muse today, a red tulip
with cherry lips open to the sun,
a chalice of daylight held up
to my thirsty mouth.

Another day she comes as the moon,
large marble making arcs above,
giving herself away until she's gone,
then returns, becoming seed
and slowly sending white blooms
into the night again.

Tomorrow she might arrive
on thunderous waves of the sea,
brine in my eyes and throat
or the soft caverns of shells strewn
on shore, a reminder
of the places I long to dwell

and one day she might land,
yellow bird on a branch,
her song calling me to look up,
glimpse the space between
her notes where the song lives,
where the silence speaks all
I need to hear.

Poetry on Four Paws
(or Arf Poetica)

Eyes alert, nose up, you catch the scent,
a thread that leads you across fields
you might never have crossed.

Simple rhythms suffice:
sleep, eat, walk, listen, smell,
present to each moment's need.

Running through snow,
you, black on white,
words tumble onto the page.

Saints
and
Animals

Heron's Virtue

"Let no one think it ridiculous to learn a lesson in virtue from birds." —St. Cuthbert

I once spent winter watching
a blue heron stand solitary at the edge
of land and sea, her thin grace, erect.
I'd wait for the moment she lifted into flight,
her long toes pushing away from solid earth
into freshets of air where wind spread
the cloak of her wings over frothy waves,
a kite, a sail, a promise.

The low December sun conspired
to turn her into gold and then just a glimmer
of gray vanishing on the horizon,
my own heart soaring above the sea
seeking a place to land again,
how the blue above embraced her form
until she was no longer bird and sky,
but ascension, a doorway.

St. Dympna and the Horse

St. Dympna and the Horse

She escapes her father's
hungry grasp and gaze,
walks days under sapphire sky,
sun a squeezed-out orange,
mouth full of dust,
feet flinch from so many steps,
seeks a place to rest and linger.

Her horse walks by her side,
never wavers, ivory pillar legs,
wide back, brown eyes scan ahead,
then his foot catches on a stone,
stumbles briefly, pulls back firmly.

In that spot water rushes up
beneath his hoof, first spray,
then fountain and Dympna
is overcome, dances
under the cool stream's surge,
splashes her friend playfully,
drinks, trembles, drops
to her knees. Knows
this ground is holy,
this water holy.
And she's been longing to enter
the door
her equine companion
has opened.

Ravens

They gather one by one,
glossy coal-colored feathers,
long cone beaks peck
at seeds I scattered,
dark eyes alert,
they arrive expectant,
pigeons and starlings depart
to make way for sounds
of squaws and caws.

Legend says St. Benedict's life
was saved by a raven.
Elijah and St. Paul
in the hungry wild
each had raven friends
bring them bread.
Someone once told me
if you feed the ravens
they bring you gifts.

I discover the truth of this
each morning as they save me
with their full-throated
presence, sometimes
jackdaws and magpies come
too, but mostly the ravens arrive
with dark thick wings,
to revel in being fed
and make their voices heard.

Holy Cow

Some days I envy St. Brigid's
devoted white cow
standing firm in the field,
wide nose sniffing the air,
endless milk for a hungry world.

If only I could stand
four-legged, day after day
while deep inside
an alchemy of rain,
grass, and clover unfolds.

I'd trade all my doubts
for hooves and horns, to know
no matter how I spend my days,
generosity wells up without
even my needing to try.

St. Brigid and the Oystercatchers

St. Brigid and the Oystercatchers

She runs fierce and swift
while men give chase
heart beating wildly
until she reaches water's edge
and can go no more.

Hearing their angry shouts
of menace on the wind,
she falls to soft sand,
lets gravity receive her
until her breath slows
and she feels at one with the sea.

Oystercatchers circle overhead,
an apparition in white and black
orange bills gather dillisk,
carragheen, algae,
create a wild blanket of green
and rust until she vanishes
and becomes the shore.

The men run past,
mistake the gentle rise and fall
under a pile of seaweed and grass
for the rhythm of the sea
and Brigid sits up slowly,
the birds encircle her,
nibble on winkles and limpets,
a seaside feast of communion.

Her eyes fill with large drops
that splash from wet lashes,
then comes laughter rising
from her gut, weeping and joy
together like a song
as they land on her
shoulders, arms, and hands.

Sometimes we have to yield
our bodies fully to earth's embrace,
to taste the end so near
to feel hope slip away like a boat
across sea's foam surface,
before we can feel the truth again
of how things hidden
can become a revelation
and heaven is there in the cries
of birds, among waves and sand.

Book of Kells

Back arched over vellum,
a swan feather soars
from between his fingers,
skin stained with ochre,
verdigris, indigo,
iron gall, gypsum.

Lost daily in the luminosity
of words, lines float in spirals
and loops, take flight
like starlings then land
on a page, acrobats
curled in on themselves.

He draws his candle closer
as night widens around him,
sweat drops splash
down, he transforms them
into a mythic beast peering
from behind a letter.

Ink and blood together,
scribing mind and heart.
For hundreds of years
to follow, pilgrims gather
to lose themselves
in his alphabet of grace,
the way words offer maps
and a glimpse of the road ahead.

St. Columba and the Crane

St. Columba and the Crane

The saint has a vision,
a crane battered by wind and rain
would tumble onto Iona's shores
in three turns of sun and moon,
the third hour before evening.

Indeed at the appointed time
she slumps her long slender
body across grass still soaked
from storm, down fluttering,
her voice strained, then silent.

Columba sends a monk to greet her,
gather her tenderly into his strong
solid arms, lift her all hollow bone
and white feathers, welcome
this weary one into the hearth.

Crane comes as pilgrim
buffeted by elements into exile,
a stranger at the door,
three days later, renewed, revived,
enough time for resurrection,

she lifts her wide wings gently
at first, then with greater force
to carry herself back across sea
and threshold, her flight
a prayer of homecoming.

St. Columba and His Horse

The old man hobbles down the road
toward the monastery gate,
rests on a roadside stone,
hears clip-clopping of hooves approach
and his faithful companion arrive.

The horse nuzzles Columba's shoulder,
shudders all down his white length
eyes glisten round and brown,
great teardrops pool and drop
sounding like rainfall.

Columba rests his forehead
against the horse's broad skull,
closes his eyes and each imagines
the other, galloping together across
heather and buttercups.

The horse knows his dear friend
will soon be leaving and mourns
this coming loss, his hoof
scrapes the ground, tries to write
a word of goodbye,

then takes wildflowers in his teeth,
extends them to the saint, as if to say
his life was full of beauty and color,
but the petals are already wilting
in the summer sun.

The wisdom of the old sages rings,
"remember you will die" and on another day
this would prompt Columba to celebrate
the gift of a new morning, but today
death is as close as the horse's warm nostrils,

he knows everything must
come to an end, even this love.
Columba rests there a long while
lets his cloak be soaked with tears,
breathing in scent of fur and fields.

St. Francis and the Wolf

The city trembled at the wolf
outside its gates, fangs
fierce, howling with hunger,
fur thick with blood.

Francis approaches softly,
palms open. When the wolf lunges
his breath stays slow and steady,
looks with eyes of love,

smiles and bows
and the beast whimpers,
licks the monk's salty face,
tail a brown banner waving,

and follows Francis
through the streets
like an old friend,
to the wonder of all.

Except perhaps it's not
such a wonder that
when we open the gate
to all that is fierce

and fearful inside us,
when we hold our hands
like begging bowls,
our hearts like candles,

the wolf within will want
to lay its soft head
upon our laps and we see
there is no more wolf and me

just one wild love,
one wild hunger.

St. Francis and the Grasshopper

St. Francis and the Grasshopper

Snow falls heavy and silent,
a lake of white flakes,
Francis peers out the window,
time for night prayer,
his brothers still tucked
away in their beds.

He steps out into drifts
which reach his knees,
breathes in the icy air,
makes puffs of smoke,
arrives at the chapel
and sits and waits.

The heavy door opens
just an inch, two green
antennae wave gently,
then large dark eyes appear,
long slender legs
and a soft swirl of snow.

Francis smiles at this friend
who leaps from the doorway
to land right beside him,
rubs her legs together
to create music for the psalms.
He sings along off-key.

They sit together a long time
in both song and silence.

After a while they depart
leaving tracks in the snow,
from the arcs and loops, you can tell
they each danced their way home.

St. Brendan and the Birds

Imagine the hubris, searching for the Saint-promised island,
the stubbornness to continue for seven journeys around the sun.
Each day on the rolling sea, his fellow monks
jostled and tossed by waves.

Brendan asks late one evening:
How will I know when I find what I seek?
Easter Sunday brings liturgy on the back of a whale,
but as if that weren't miracle enough, they travel onward.

The ship is tossed onto sand and stone.
they look up to behold a broad and magnificent
oak frosted with white birds hiding the branches entirely,
downy tree limbs reaching upward.

The monks stand huddled under a blue stone sky
relieved to be on stable earth for now.
The sun descends, Vespers, rose to lavender to violet,
heralding the great night's arrival.

They release a collective sigh of contentment, the air expands
around them as a thousand snowy birds ascend into that
newly hollowed space, and throats open together,
a human-avian chorus of shared devotion to the ancient songs
and ways.

Ever eager to journey forward, Brendan still lingers for fifty days
sitting in that oak cathedral, feathers scribing their own sacred texts.
In those moments, did the relentless seeking fall away,
sliding off like the veil hiding a bride's expectant face?

St. Melangell and the Hare

St. Melangell and the Hare

Melangell sails the Irish sea
to the wilds of Wales,
flees a marriage and seeks time
alone among a storm of hawthorn,
feeds on hazelnuts and dandelions,
gathers lady's mantle each morning
to sip their dew, plunges her hands
in the river, freezing and fresh,
sleeps on moss in the cave-close stone,
delights at birdsong, seeks
the sacred in hunger and rain.

One warm day, her quiet disrupted,
hot breath of men and hounds
approach, jaws wide.
Teeth gleam, foam sputters,
tails swish as they scrabble
for a hare with brown legs
bounding, a great roar of wet fur
and whiskers –
           the hare leaps
into the folds of Melangell's cloak.

Defiant stands the saint,
draws a circle around herself.
Dogs and men can go no further.

Melangell strokes the hare's ears,
soothes his clanging heart,
whispers *you are safe now*

as howls recede on the wind
and the valley becomes sanctuary.

You can still glimpse it
on sun-sparkled days when bluebells
sway and oak leaves rustle
from squirrel-scurry-scamper
and you take the soft hare
of your life into your arms,
whisper into those long ears
blessings all down her trembling
length and remind her that
she too no longer needs to run.

St. Ciaran and His First Monks

Ciaran seeks solace and silence,
sits under a wide tree, watches leaves
transform into fluttering jewels,
basks in stippled sunlight,
waits on flapping wings of birds
to lift his thoughts to sky.
A fierce boar arrives with heart
softened by saint's gentleness,
gathers twigs and straw,
builds Ciaran a cell.
As winter arrives, others gather too:
fox and badger, wolf and deer,
together they write poems on bark
and stone, howl songs of praise
at dawn's doorway
and dusk's sweet leaving.
Legend says they became the monk's
first disciples, but Ciaran knows better.
These teachers sing of the sacred
better than any book, his prayer
is to just wait and watch,
learn the wisdom of wild grace.

St. Julian and the Cat

St. Julian and the Cat

Stone by stone the wall grew
until her cell was sealed,
light blocked except for
three small windows —
    one for sacrament
    another, food and waste
    a third to give guidance.

Each day brought dozens to her
praying for their sick and dead,
night became time of solace
and silence, she could not
sleep long in the damp,
pulled wool close around her
as she sighed into the dark,
relief at quiet moments.

Then came mewing,
leaping, pouncing, the cat
left there to catch rats,
at first annoyed at disruption
she soon found wisdom
in his aim and purpose,
grace in his hours of stillness,
how she too was there to hunt
the holy, and rest into being.

Morning prayers became
a mix of chants and purrs
as warm fur nestles into her lap.

Visitors arrive again
to her window, she gives
her most sage advice:

54   *allow yourself to be comforted,*
       do not be afraid of the night,
       and pursue what you long for
       with a love that is fierce.

St. Marvan and the White Boar

The holy man wanders the forest,
in search of a place he can hear
pine needles drop, and seeds
crack open each spring.

A white boar, said to be
his muse, joins him,
calls forth songs and poems
daily from the hermit's heart.

Does he find inspiration
in how the beast's nostrils
steam with each breath,
send up clouds of longing?

Or how the boar's long tusks
slice through thicket
and gleam like sunlight
pouring from its face?

Or how it roots
in underearth for hidden
things, bringing back gifts
as if they were jewels?

Or the way the boar's fierce face
softens each time the monk places
a hand on its brow, wiry and coarse,
when others had always pulled back?

St. Paul and the Lions

St. Paul and the Lions

His throat dry as the desert
which embraced him
a hundred years, the hermit
finally breathes his last
at the sand's hot edge.

Anthony arrives to find his friend
gone into the great night,
sits vigil all day until the sky
is covered in bruises,
weeps a river into the dust.

From shadows emerge two lions,
great golden paws and claws dig
a deep hole and roar with grief,
lower the monk's body into riven earth
and stand together in silence

until the dawn cracks apart
and sparrows sing the world awake,
until both human and animal
standing on the unsteady ground
that will one day claim them

come to know only two things
as solid:
death, like iron, immovable

and companionship.
A communion of creatures ready
to join in our lament for all
that has been lost, waiting
with us for all that is coming home again.

St. Ailbhe and the Wolf

A baby left in the forest
cries from hunger,
tiny mouth making "o"s
of longing into air.
A wolf approaches,
her cold snout nuzzles
soft pink skin,
wraps her silver body
around him, offers fur
and milk as gift.

Months go by, the boy
grows strong and steady,
wolf teaches the hunt.
He wakes to dawn's
daily song of wind
and warbler, respects
night's mysteries,
becomes a holy man,
eyes always stalking God
in badger, beech, and bees.

One day he leaves
the woods to serve the world,
becomes a bishop,
but when conventions start
to confine him, his eyes glint
with wildness, and on nights
when the moon emerges
from her sleep-dark cave

he slips away to the meadow
behind the church,
tilts his head back
and lets loose
his most guttural howl.

St. Gall and the Bear

St. Gall and the Bear

An Irish monk on a mission
saunters through Swiss forest,
where a bear – fur bristling,
nostrils dark and large – charges him.
The holy man does not clench,
extends his hand like a slowly
opening peony, chunk of bread
in his palm, offers it to those
long-clawed paws which take it eagerly
into hungry jaws and lumber off.

The bear returns that evening,
wood piled high in brown arms
to build the monk a fire.
Together they sit for hours,
listen to night's music,
count stars as they appear,
bask in ember's warmth

When the great bear of your life
charges toward you, nourish it
with the bread of your kindness.
When it comes carrying kindling,
sit down with it, see what is sparked
and what shapes dance in the flame.

Ross Errilly Friary

A plague draped the land
in black loss, carved new
hollows, summoned wailing
from the four directions

until an angel came
in a dream: *build*
a sanctuary, go west
until you see the sign.

They walk toward
the sun's descent, orange
blaze perched on the horizon
then dark like the inside of a crow,

monks rest among granite
and hawthorn by the Black River,
hear its song in the darkness,
follow its flow into night

until the moment when
before the sun emerges again
three swans rise up
into the violet sky

a vision in white and feathers
holding clusters of flax
in their bright bills,
they circle once,
    twice,
        three times overhead,

the monks follow
beneath their airy rounds,
find a thousand purple
blooms in midwinter.

Sometimes we have to listen,
follow a dream into darkness,
a trail of stars
that vanishes behind us,

allow ourselves to be swallowed,
to feel the widening
of our wings, our petals
flare open.

St. Gobnait and the Bees

St. Gobnait and the Bees

She treasures their golden gift,
mixing herbs to make medicine
for sisters with coughs,
guests with aches,
even the itchy Abbey dog.

She measures carefully
not wasting a drop,
each spoonful labor of hours.
Her bees love her too,
she leaves plenty
for them when she gathers
purple heads of clover,
yellow dandelion faces,
yarrow's tiny white blooms.
She does not need to reach,
just waits for wind
to bend blossoms toward her,
accepts their offering with thanks,
marvels each summer day
how quickly the plants grow
as if gulping down moonlight
all night. Morning dew
offers another elixir.

One quiet day cattle rustlers
come and Gobnait nods
to her buzzing friends
who quickly swarm and sting,
swiftly restore the sanctuary,

then return to savor sweetness
hiding under each petal
for those who know where to look.

St. Kevin and the Otters

The saint rises early
to sing the sun aloft,
watch sky drip pink paint.
Birds tweet psalms with him,
trees tremble the refrain.
Otters glide through the lake,
slip smoothly onto shore,
salmon in their mouths,
a gift for the monk.

Each day they feast
on wisdom together,
saint and swimmers,
each night they dream
salmon dreams of slicing
upstream, scanning
with silver eyes, like coins
at the bottom of the well,
wishes waiting for a future

moment, when hungry again
for kinship they light the fire
to warm and transform,
sit together and be nourished
for the many cold days ahead.

St. Kevin Holds Open His Hand

Imagine being like Kevin.
Your grasping fist softens,
fingers uncurl and
palms open, rest upward,
and the blackbird
weaves twigs and straw and bits of string
in the bowl of your hand,
you feel the delicate weight of
speckled blue orbs descend,
and her feathered warmth
settling in.

How many days can you stay,
   open,
waiting
for the shell
to fissure and crack,
awaiting the slow emergence
of tiny gaping mouths
and slick wings
that need time to strengthen?

Are you willing to wait and watch?
Not to withdraw your
affections too soon?
Can you fall in love with the
exquisite ache in your arms
knowing the hatching it holds?

Can you stay not knowing
how broad those wings will
become, or how they will fly
awkwardly at first,
then soar above you

until you have become the sky
and all that remains is
your tiny shadow
swooping across the earth.

St. Cuthbert and the Otters

St. Cuthbert and the Otters

The saint stands immersed in the North Sea,
his nightly vigil, waves lap his beard,
offers prayers of wildness and wakefulness,
the moon is a communion wafer
floating across sky.
He smiles as curious seals swim past,
when dawn approaches, birds open
their beaks in song, land on his shoulders.

Each morning he steps back onto shore
with wrinkled toes, skin pale blue,
two otters scurry over,
warm him with fish-hued breath,
wrap themselves around his frigid feet,
until he can wiggle them again,

they beckon him to romp and frolic
and in the midst of this otter-saint
rumble-rumpus, lost in laughter,
he forgets himself, forgets the many
names of God, realizes
this too is a kind of prayer.

St. Columbanus in the Forest

St. Columbanus in the Forest

He learned long ago
he doesn't have to seek out
wild things, only rest and wait,
when his heart is full
he starts to sing until
birds twitter and trapeze
branch to branch,
land tiny feet on his shoulders,
brush his bristly face.

Squirrels dizzy with delight,
maelstrom of scamper and bustle
to climb his thin arms,
their giggling red heads
peer from folds of his robe
as if playing a secret game
meant only for them,
only for those who believe
such things are possible.

St. Macarius and the Hyena

She pads softly into
the holy man's cave,
rests her paw on his arm,
tugs his tunic;
her brown eyes
plead, his eyes green
with kindness.

He follows her, finds
her cubs all blind from birth,
heals them and sets
them free to see
what they could only
smell and feel before,
how their eyes squint at first
in bright summer light.
Their mother's spotted fur
encircles them as they strain
to look upward to branches
drawing stencils against the sky.

She had to find a way to thank him
in proportion to this gift,
brings him sheepskin
more lavish than anything
the poor monk owned.
The man who had slept on stone
nestles in and dreams
of ways to see the new again.

St. Clare and the Cat

She reclines with a sigh,
an ache spreads through her,
she knows she must not fight
this time of rest,
reaches for her yarn
which slips from her hands
across the stone floor
spinning like the cosmos.

Her cat, waiting for a moment
like this, pounces on
the fleeing fleece,
bats the ball of blue
between paws,
as it unravels,
tangles around his tail,
the saint can't help but laugh,
grateful for the levity
of forgetting herself,

and the yarn
is back in her hands
in a flash. The cat settles
his warm ribs into her lap
and watches closely
as she begins
to weave new worlds
from wool and joy.

The Swifts Preach to St. Clare

The Swifts Preach to St. Clare*

She awakens as black sky cracks apart
sending out violet streamers, the swifts
descend from above, tiny seraphim
swimming across the dazzle of dawn.
She watches for hours with sapphire eyes,
head back, *alleluia* fills her mouth
like sweet wine from the hills below,
they swoop and circle again and again
trailing halos overhead, her tears
tumble splashing her dress,
bells call her to church, but she knows
her prayers have already begun.

When late summer comes bursting
with gold and juice, she blesses
the birds' leaving, always pilgrims,
learns to let them go for now
and when Sister Death at last
arrives to claim her, Clare
becomes those wings she cherished,
rising and resting on currents of love.

This story is still being scribed
across sky in feathers and desire.
One sun-glazed morning with your feet
rooted in dark soil let your gaze ascend,
feel your longing to be lifted,
your hunger to be
carried home again.

---

* This is the only one of the saints and animals poem series that is not based on a story that already exists about the saint. The poem was inspired by a personal visit to Assisi for retreat and pilgrimage.

Myths and Fairy Tales

Once Upon a Time

There is a country named Wonder
where each night your passport
is stamped with scent of lilacs

still wet from the storm.
When the border guard asks
the purpose of your visit,

you only need open your eyes wide,
leave your suitcases behind
and step with naked feet

onto grass still damp with dew.
There is no yesterday or tomorrow,
only a place called Here

and it rises like an amaryllis,
tastes like first bite of summer strawberry,
until the alarm bell rings

and you are in bed again
with a choice to make
about how to embrace this day.

What She Does Not Know
(for unsuspecting Selkies†everywhere)

She does not know there is a reason
she always feels out of place
her life rigid and small, like living in a doll's house
a marriage more trap than longing
and when she chokes on courtesy and convention
the salt which burns her throat is not just tears.

She does not know that when she stands
on the sea's wild edge and can finally
breathe, dream, weep,
her body strains forward
seawater in her veins, barnacles behind her knees
waves lap her ankles, thighs, torso, her cold breasts.

She does not know that when she swims
in that wide expanse and the swell
pulls her under, she does not need to struggle,
the sea has been longing for her as well –
everyone onshore aghast –
her daughter will grieve and wail and awaken

from dreams of the deep dark water
also calling her name.

† In Scottish and Irish mythology selkies, meaning "seal folk," are mythological beings capable of changing from seal to human form by shedding their skin. A typical folk tale is that of a man who finds a female selkie on the seashore, steals her skin, and compels her to become his wife. But the wife will spend her time in captivity longing for the sea, her true home, and will often be seen gazing longingly at the ocean. She may bear several children by her human husband, but once she discovers where her husband has hidden her skin, she will immediately return to the sea and abandon the children she loved. In some accounts, her children follow her to the sea.—See Wikipedia®, "Selkie."

Selkie Song

Under the moon's wide gleam
she steps onto dry ground,
slips from her skin,
a vision in milky light.

She wants for a moment
to feel land under her feet,
to see what this solid world
offers that the sea doesn't hold.

Solidity is seductive,
can make one forget
the joys of a fluid life,
but the sea rises within

unable to resist
the swelling tide,
her search gains urgency
for the fur that could set her free.

Where has yours been buried
all these years? Check the closets,
the garage, and the jar in back
of the cupboard.

Slide it back on, fear not
the waves, your body recalls
the deep beneath the surface,
and how to swim and dive.

Little Red Riding Hood

First of all
red is so not my color
but a thrift store bargain
is nothing to scoff at
when mother has squandered
all on whiskey and lottery.

She hands me the basket
my eyes grow wide,
grandma is unwell
go straight there,
(she cautions)
her eyes narrow.

But why go to the woods
if you aren't going
to gather snowdrops
breathe in wild garlic
collect mushrooms for soup
or lichen from branches for tea?

Finally I knock on the yellow door,
scent of rose perfume mixed with fur,
she looked a hairy sight
big ears for hearing
big eyes for seeing
big mouth for eating;

knife ready under my cape
no need to be rescued
by woodsman or other,
but the wolf was
just grandma returning,
no longer afraid of anything.

Pomegranate

The meadow
opened to swallow her,
hungry for her bright eyes
and unbruised heart.

Some say she was tricked
into eating it,
I believe the moment came
when she looked upon life

with its treachery and poison,
knew it like a lover,
and it broke open a kindness
she had not known before.

No longer victim, but Queen,
a friend to winter's silence,
she welcomes swallowed souls
with their wounds and stuck screams.

When the red fruit arrives
pluck those plump seeds.
Know the fields will have to lie
resting for a time:
you will have to stay a while.

Handless Maiden I

The world conspires to sever our hands
a hundred different ways, leaves us
unable to embrace, to reach,
to tell us at least it wasn't your head,
be grateful for that.

You're still alive and allowed to roam free,
and instead of staying to live an artificial life
fed from false riches, you choose
to go into the forest,
her long branches all around you
the scent of damp earth fills your nostrils.

You somehow know once you've lost the path
you've found your way into the dark pulsing
heart of life, to the place that does not sever
but offers healing as freely as a rushing spring,
cold and brisk on a hot summer day,
and you try to drink it all but realize
there will always be more water
than you can take in.

The overflow is the point,
and you kneel down in front of it,
in your deepest bow, head tilted to earth,
hands re-grown and submerged in the icy rush;
and you remember this is what it is to be loved,
to drink from love, to swim in love
like the sea that suspends you,
to breathe it in like summer's first lilac
carried on the breeze.

Handless Maiden II

She spent seven years in the forest
and her hands, once severed
in a deal with the devil,
grew again.

We might want to know
what spells she uttered, what plants
she gathered, how hard she had to work
to achieve this regeneration.

But what if the truth is she did nothing
at all, simply yielded to wood and leaf,
came to know the robins by name,
could tell apart a dozen kinds of mosses,
just from hours of paying attention.

What if the only way to heal that deep wound
is to stop trying so hard, stop seeking
and allow yourself to be found?
Transfiguration was waiting for you
and you didn't even know.

Apple Tree

There is nothing behind the farmhouse
thought the Miller, *nothing but an old*
apple tree, let the devil have it,
how he had walked by it a thousand times
and never noticed the way its leaves shimmered
in early dawn when everything else still slept,
how I could sit for hours with my spine
lifted by its sturdy trunk, waiting for the rain
to start, how the earth smelled so much
like itself as it waited to drink,
branches home to blackbird and lichen,
ripening globes from green to red,
how she offered her fruit freely
to a hungry world, nothing expected
in return, and when I bite into one
I am suddenly Eve or Snow White
but this apple is instead the doorway
to heaven, and awakening for those who savor,
a long wordless conversation between
hunger and feasting.

Once

my hands were made of silver,
delicate, refined, needing to be polished
daily, glinting on sun-heavy days
until I made my way into the woods
listened for a long while, ear pressed to soft earth
thirsty for the song I heard
among roots and moss, rumors
that spring was coming, could even hear
the magnolia bud rumbling.

I stayed that way for years, prone,
breathing in scent of fur and feather
until everything silver fell away
until flesh rose back up my arms
pink covered me like the promise
of that song I heard, now I'm eager
for callouses and blisters,
to mottle my fingers with ink,
to touch the world as if for the first time.

Dreaming

You are dreaming
but do not know it yet,
find yourself in a locked room,
feel your way across walls, floors,
and ceiling, no margin for opening,
no cracks to release you,
you continue to reach and bang
and try to pry free anything you can
until you fall to the floor exhausted,
your hands worn down like erasers

and a piece of paper falls from your pocket
with foreign words, you scrutinize the letters
try to make sense of their shapes,
pray over the sounds they make, hoping
this is an incantation, a magic formula,
until your throat is dry and your eyes burn
and you long for rest from this endless project

and the room takes you into its wide arms
and you set aside the paper, do the only thing
you can do now which is surrender
and when you do awaken to this world
again you find bruises on your hands
and the note left by your bedside you scribbled
in the middle of the night simply reads
"tear this up," and you do even though the words
still echo and your arms still ache,
but your hands are whole again.

Solace of Wild Places

"When the Moon Comes Up"

(After Federico Garcia Lorca)

Some nights the moon rises
like a silver balloon
glinting on a glittering sea
or a white chocolate truffle
on a hungry tongue.

Some nights the moon is dark,
absent, the sky a raven's wing,
other nights the moon is just
a sliver, a fingernail, a promise.

Some nights the moon is a pomegranate,
red-stained, offering seeds.

Some nights all I can smell is jasmine
and vanilla, and the tide drawing out.

When She Despairs

(after Wendell Berry)

When she despairs, knowing how
each thing she loves will one day end,
she goes down to the river's edge,
lets otters remind her of play
salmon of perseverance
cormorant of stillness.

She watches how sun and water
create gold and silver in a flash
and forgets her worries,
suddenly sees she is swan's wings
on a winter wind, bud on the blackthorn
branch, ready to break into blossom.

Love Letter

"I prowl the woods and streams
And linger watching things themselves." —Han-Shan

Have you ever fallen in love
with a mountain, spent hours
memorizing her lines and gashes,
swooned over a scree-covered slope,
uplifted by its rise into sky
saying *I am here*, no apologies,
followed its trails, scooping clusters
of wildflowers along the way,
seen how it ascends from earth
like a great heron with wide wings,
like your own, most fervent prayer?

There is Wonder, Still

Some winter mornings
crimson ribbons float
across a slate sky,
dark cracks open
like an eggshell
and the sun is a yolk
singing in gold.

She sees those of us
leaning back
looking up at her,
mouths hanging open

and she sees those
impatient in traffic,
leaning forward
as if the whole world
had not just come alive
for a moment, as if hurry
were the only way.

Sunlight glides down
our gaping throats
while others rush by
wondering why
they are always so hungry.

"Peace Comes from Dropping Slow"
(after W. B. Yeats)

Do you count your heartbeats
hoping for a million more?
Or number your breaths, sharp and quick?
Or the steps you take across
this glorious earth?

Until one morning you see how time
is fleeting but also impossibly slow?
That time is best counted in moments:
sips of wine spreading gladness
through your limbs, blush
of breathless conversation
while embers glow, waiting
to be stoked and set aflame.

"A Glimpse of the Underglimmer"
(after Bashō)

You can see it sometimes in October
when the sun's low angle slides
gold over the field,
effervescence of light,

or you stand in a forest of cedars
and March rain pads
hundreds of tiny feet across
the emerald canopy,

or the fireflies of July form
new constellations, then vanish
into summer's night leaving only
trails of light in your memory,

or you stand in a May meadow,
a fox crossing quietly, you hold
still as possible, the sliver of moon
above, holding its breath with you.

Spring Mysteries

Could it be that trees are sung into blooming
each spring as birds gather open-throated
on their long dark branches?

Or perhaps it is the birds who only sing
once they feel the branches humming
beneath their tiny feet?

And what of me? Do I sing because the world
is impossibly in blossom? Or do I flower
because I hear the ancient song?

Always

It is always dawn somewhere
on this forever turning earth
eyes just now opening.

It is always midday someplace,
sun at its peak,
all of life illuminated.

It is always dusk somewhere,
sweet leaving of day
asking us to embrace the end.

It is always midnight someplace,
ten thousand dreams
erupting into the darkness.

Spring Ephemerals

The lambs have appeared overnight
smelling of salt and soil.
Where just yesterday bellies were
still heavy with growth,
soft mouths suckle,
so full of longing, tiny circles of joy.

Sparrows form a choir,
coax the sun awake,
thrum of blackthorn blossoms
where before was only branch and bud.
A yellow festival of daisies and dandelions
blankets a fragrant meadow,
swaths of primrose announce themselves
with pink fanfare.

The river reveals she is my sister
as she rushes into the arms of the sea.
White horses galloping across sky
are my brothers, and soon I see even
the delicate bone left from a swallow
as part of me, white gleam of belonging,
how I am no longer Earth-and-me
but one wild love for this world.

Summer Breezes

I lie down in the long grass
face to the blue platter serving up the sky
riveted by starlings flapping fiercely,
how hard it can be to bear my weight

but today I think of the pear
waiting on the table
inside the cool dark kitchen,
a perfect orb of sweetness,

and wildflowers sway all around me
as if there is some impossible song they all hear
and when the breeze visits all they can do is dance
and wonder why I don't do the same.

Nocturne

Sometimes I awaken at night
although still in a dream
and the air around me is violet.
Here in the heart of the forest
I am elegance of swan,
fierceness of bear,
sweetness of squirrel,
I am all these things under
night's generous embrace,
how the moon, a broken dinner plate
has the courage to soar
how my prayers for the world grow
more intense and I wonder
what of this grace will still
be left by morning?

The Wild Self

Into the Forest

Come to the forest, I hear the whisper
but I delay, so many tasks ahead
a list as long as the highway,
the engine of doing so loud.

Come to the forest, she teases
but I delay, afraid of the dark,
of the hundred kinds of mosses
the beasts hiding in hollows.

Come to the forest, she insists
but I delay, wanting to locate maps
that chart the way, find my compass,
fill my pack with essentials.

Come to the forest, she still cries,
the reasons not to go are so many
and I look back on them
floating behind me like smoke,

even as I lower my head
to pass under branches,
place bare feet on quiet earth
and find a place to rest

eyes close and I am there
among ash and elder,
hawthorn and yew, all singing
welcome: at last.

Crossing the Divide

She walks, as if from a dream, into your life,
ribboned hair unraveling, brown eyes
like cups of tea, come to whisper
a secret into your trembling ear.

You try hard not to listen, clinging
to your calendar, your achievements,
your loneliness, until the silver ache
of it all spreads through your limbs

and she holds out her hand across
the ravine, and you see how the chasm
is not empty, but filled with a rushing
river, and you can swim until

you become fish and flow, until
you are the ancient stream
emerging from stone,
until her face becomes yours.

Autobiography

She loves winter and the rain
only drinks coffee with cream and sugar
feels happiest in the forest
but loves living in the city
thinks dogs are small wonders
hides in the shade on sunny days
feeds crows outside her apartment window
has three tattoos, all of which hurt
wishes her hair were gray
sees her father's feet when she removes her socks
her head too big for one-size-fits-all
hates having her ears touched
orphaned at the age of thirty-three
swims to feel the water hold her.

"Things I Didn't Know I Loved"
(after Nazim Hikmet)

I never knew how much I loved
heavy rain on a Sunday morning
curled in bed with coffee
a Morse code tapping the windows
telling me I have no reason to leave.

I didn't realize how much I adored
peonies until one May afternoon
I spent four hours photographing
the bouquet (you brought me
for no reason) on our dining table.

I never knew how much I cherished
the alchemy taking place in kitchens
until I mixed wheat and yeast together,
felt it sticky in my hands,
and from the oven emerged bread.

I didn't know how much I loved
this sagging body of mine,
until one day the mirror showed
me not scars and marks, but a story
of what it means to endure.

I never knew how much I loved
the forest until I walked so far
and so long my arms were coated
with moss and my life became
a fairy tale written in the snow.

Where Are You From?

I stumble over this pleasantry each time,
born in Manhattan, raised among
steel spires and yellow cabs, parents
long dead, no siblings either,
West Coast dweller for twenty-one years,
first in San Francisco, foggy summers
and bridges in every direction,
Seattle beckoned with forests
and sea, I learned to love the rain,
until Europe called, Vienna
where my father's ashes are buried,
red streetcars, imperial presence,
finally to Galway, Ireland,
on the edge of the Atlantic, fierce winds
each winter and rain that buckets
and lashes, stories by the fire,
stones that hold prayers and sing,
far from American shores,
the Otherworld so close.

Wittgenstein in Connemara

I turn north off the N59
bog on one side, Lough Fee
on the other, turn right at Lough Muck,
over the hill, along the peninsula,
to the end of the road at Rosroe Pier,
mouth of Killary Fjord, edge of the known
world, all gorse and heather and sea,
Mweelrae sleeps across the way.

He certainly didn't belong there,
Austrian philosopher turned
Cambridge professor, a hermit
seeking dark quiet around himself
for thoughts to ripen, what must
the locals have made of him? His slim
figure, austere, mannered,
bird-tamer, holding out his hands
full of breadcrumbs and seed,
smiling as sparrows land
on tiny feet, letting the blackbird
teach him about patience,
perhaps seeking the God
for whom he had no words.

Not how the world is, is the mystical,
but that it is, he once said. At night
I stand under an ample sky
and can't help but agree, I dream
he is there with me, I fix him tea
and say I don't understand his writing,

he laughs gently, asks for sugar,
we sit together in the long quiet
broken only by the soft voice of flames
in the wood stove and the rain
that has started thrumming the window.

Every Day Has Its Dog

Dog of Monday
    rolls in grass, legs flail like salmon in a cage
Dog of Tuesday
    bows deep before me, calls for frolic
Dog of Wednesday
    wet nose directs my hand to fur, chin, ears, belly
Dog of Thursday
    curls nose to toe, black crescent on blue blanket
Dog of Friday
    dreams of the chase, taste of feathers on sleeping tongue
Dog of Saturday
    tail wags at homecoming, a tiny flag in heavy wind
Dog of Sunday
    leans against me, sighs, eyes large and brown.

Welcome Home

I return home from the shop,
armful of cheese, bread, flowers,
you greet me there at the door
your body a dolphin making arcs
out of the sea,
your tail a metronome of gladness,
you look at me with eyes color
of dark earth pleading,
tongue, a pink peony petal,
licorice nose, sour apple breath,
you roll onto your back,
belly an invitation
telling me I am forgiven
for leaving you behind,
telling me to stay here with you
for a long while.

Faith

All night the marigolds stand vigil,
wait for the sun to return again,
its rise and peak and dip again each day,
its arc of warmth and light
showers the yellow petals
until sun and flower are one.

I wish I had their faith on storm-rattled days,
where dawn to dusk is blown gray and soaked,
that consolation awaits,
that when clouds lift, the vigorous joy
that comes will shake me free of myself.

Closing

My Last Poem
(after Br. Paul Quenon)

My last poem will
savor your warm hand
pressed into mine, my other hand
resting on the dog's wiry fur,
chest rising and falling,
she rolls over to display her belly
telling me I am not done quite yet.

My last poem will look around
the room, full of many unread books,
and I will finally be able to rest into
all that is unfinished, the dishes
still piled by the sink from our
last dinner together, hearing
the clink of glasses, friends asking
for more asparagus, knowing
there is so much more than food here.

My last poem will see
a vase of yellow tulips on the table,
a single petal falling, a golden bowl of gladness
welcoming its slow demise,
and the open window.

A Door Opens

onto the moonless night,
rectangle of light spills
into the dark cathedral,
an arc of silence spreads
through winter wind,
leaves abandon branches.

Somewhere a spiral of crows
settles onto those bony arms
fattened hedgehogs go to sleep,
dream of spring-plump
worms and slugs.

I stand at the doorway,
feel the pull between
inside burrowed under blankets,
fire glow and candles,

and stepping out under stars
onto frost-solid earth
which whispers of gifts waiting,
like the seeds that rest,
like the squirrel finding a hollow
of nuts after many hungry nights
like the first lavender light
that reminds me
how much is possible.

The following poems had versions previously published in the following books and journals:

"St. Brendan and the Birds" first appeared in *Illuminating the Way: Embracing the Wisdom of Monks and Mystics*, Ave Maria Press, 2016.

"St. Kevin Holds Open His Hand" first appeared in *Skylight 47* and in *The Soul's Slow Ripening: Celtic Wisdom for Discernment*, Ave Maria Press 2018.

"What She Does Not Know" first appeared in *Tales from the Forest*.

"Raven," "St. Brigid and the Oystercatchers," "Holy Cow," and "St. Hildegard Gives Her Writing Advice" first appeared in *U.S. Catholic*.

"St. Melangell and the Hare," "I Greet the Muse," and "Spring Ephemerals" first appeared in *Bearings*, the online journal of the Collegeville Institute.

"You Are Here" first appeared in *Presence: Journal of Catholic Poetry*.

"When the Moon Comes Up" first appeared in *The Blue Nib*.

"Aubade" and "Once Upon a Time" first appeared in *Anchor*.

"Handless Maiden," "Where Are You From?," "Every Day Has Its Dog," "Crossing the Divide," "Peace Comes from Dropping Slow," "Things I Didn't Know I Loved," "Wittgenstein in Connemara," "Love Letter," "Nocturne," and "Poetry on Four Paws" first appeared in *impspired* online journal.

"Ross Errilly Friary" first appeared in *Crannog*.

"Pomegranate" first appeared in *Three Drops from a Cauldron*.

"There is Wonder, Still" first appeared in *The Anglican Theological Review*.

"Book of Kells" first appeared in *Arts*.

"St. Gobnait and the Bees," "St. Columba and the Horse," "St. Marvan and the White Boar," and "St. Dympna and the Horse" first appeared in *Saint Katherine Review*.

"Once" first appeared in *North West Words*.

"Little Red Riding Hood" first appeared in *Bangor Journal*.

"St. Gall and the Bear" first appeared in *Crossways Journal*.

About Paraclete Press

Who We Are

As the publishing arm of the Community of Jesus, Paraclete Press presents a full expression of Christian belief and practice—from Catholic to Evangelical, from Protestant to Orthodox, reflecting the ecumenical charism of the Community and its dedication to sacred music, the fine arts, and the written word. We publish books, recordings, sheet music, and video/DVDs that nourish the vibrant life of the church and its people.

What We Are Doing

Books

PARACLETE PRESS BOOKS show the richness and depth of what it means to be Christian. While Benedictine spirituality is at the heart of who we are and all that we do, our books reflect the Christian experience across many cultures, time periods, and houses of worship.

We have many series, including *Paraclete Essentials*; *Paraclete Fiction*; *Paraclete Poetry*; *Paraclete Giants*; and for children and adults, *All God's Creatures*, books about animals and faith; and *San Damiano Books*, focusing on Franciscan spirituality. Others include *Voices from the Monastery* (men and women monastics writing about living a spiritual life today), *Active Prayer*, and new for young readers: *The Pope's Cat*. We also specialize in gift books for children on the occasions of Baptism and First Communion, as well as other important times in a child's life, and books that bring creativity and liveliness to any adult spiritual life.

The MOUNT TABOR BOOKS series focuses on the arts and literature as well as liturgical worship and spirituality; it was created in conjunction with the Mount Tabor Ecumenical Centre for Art and Spirituality in Barga, Italy.

Music

PARACLETE PRESS DISTRIBUTES RECORDINGS of the internationally acclaimed choir *Gloriæ Dei Cantores*, the *Gloriæ Dei Cantores Schola*, and the other instrumental artists of the *Arts Empowering Life Foundation*.

PARACLETE PRESS IS THE EXCLUSIVE NORTH AMERICAN DISTRIBUTOR for the Gregorian chant recordings from St. Peter's Abbey in Solesmes, France. Paraclete also carries all of the Solesmes chant publications for Mass and the Divine Office, as well as their academic research publications.

In addition, PARACLETE PRESS SHEET MUSIC publishes the work of today's finest composers of sacred choral music, annually reviewing over 1,000 works and releasing between 40 and 60 works for both choir and organ.

Video

Our video/DVDs offer spiritual help, healing, and biblical guidance for a broad range of life issues including grief and loss, marriage, forgiveness, facing death, understanding suicide, bullying, addictions, Alzheimer's, and Christian formation.

Learn more about us at our website: www.paracletepress.com or phone us toll-free at 1.800.451.5006

SCAN TO READ

You may also be interested in...

Dreaming of Stones
Poems

Christine Valters Paintner

ISBN 978-1-64060-108-6
$18 | Trade paperback

The poems in *Dreaming of Stones* are about what endures: hope and desire, changing seasons, wild places, love, and the wisdom of mystics. Inspired by the poet's time living in Ireland, these readings invite you into deeper ways of seeing the world. Drawing on her commitment as a Benedictine oblate, the poems arise out of sitting in silence and practicing *lectio divina*, in which life becomes the holy text. In her first exclusively poetic collection, Christine writes with a contemplative heart about kinship with nature, ancestral connections, intimacy, the landscape, the unfolding nature of time, and Christian mystics. This volume can be read for reflection to spark the heart and to offer solace and inspiration in difficult times.

"Christine Valters Paintner's poems have both a mystical and an earthy sensibility to them, drawing us to the transcendent as well as the immanent presence of the divine. Her poems, much like her nonfiction writing, offer the reader an experience of retreat and sacred encounter."
—**Richard Rohr**, OFM

Available at bookstores
Paraclete Press | 1-800-451-5006
www.paracletepress.com